ENDORSEMENTS

I have known David for over 10 years now, and have grown to respect his unique and much-needed insight all the more throughout the changing seasons of my career and ministry. God has given David a gift of wisdom and the ability to accurately identify salient points in almost any situation, challenging the believer to be a more effective leader not only in the Church but in the marketplace. Having personally been in full-time evangelistic ministry within the church for many years, and now owning a successful business in the marketplace, David has been a key member of my team along the way and has consistently pointed me to live out my calling in more effective ways. This brief and succinct book is a wonderful encapsulation of the challenge every believer is called to live out, whether within church ministry or the marketplace. I highly encourage anyone who takes Jesus' calling to make disciples seriously to take a few moments and read David's words, hear his heart, and be challenged to pursue God's best within their vocation. You won't be disappointed!

—**Christer Tepper, Owner**
Import Paint & Body Company
Charlotte, North Carolina

No greater friend will a local church Pastor find than David, a man filled with Godly wisdom that has come from a lifetime of walking in faith. For the few bold leaders willing to be challenged by God's Word as we enter one of the most turbulent times in Biblical History, Dr. David Paul Robinson will take us back to the roots of the Great Commission. This book is a must-read for every leader no matter their title or position to learn clear principles to prepare God's people in their Ministry calling in both the church and marketplace. If you have never read one of Dr. Robinson's books, you will be blessed and surprised to learn things you never learned in Bible School or Seminary. Let the coach take you to the next level, your ministry will be more fruitful and powerful in transforming your community, city, and the nations as you put into practice these Biblical truths.

—Keith Lawler, Missionary
Southeast Asia
Since 2004
Chicago, Illinois

Well, David Robinson has done it again! Questioning the church 'process,' which has clearly been ineffective for decades, and offering a solution that challenges the status quo. The early church changed the known world, not by huddling within the four walls of a building, but in the blacksmith shops, food markets, and wharves where believers, who had a Great Commission conscience, were engaged every day. It is time to leave our comfort zone and get back to the Biblical model of being salt and light where it is needed most.

—Chuck Moore, Founding Pastor
Tree Of Life Ministries
Marion, Indiana

Love the book and the heart of your message. It is a challenge for us who know something needs to be done in our world today, and a plan for those looking to make the changes needed. It's our wake up call, reminding us greater Kingdom work lies ahead.

—Dr. Daryl Merrill, Jr.
Pastor, Christian Life Church
VP, Christian Life College
Mt. Prospect, Illinois

All of David's writings that have crossed my desk since our first meeting in 1978 have been excellent. I rate this as one of his best. The ultimate purpose of the Church is to bring honor and glory to its head, Jesus Christ. It does this as it fulfills its purpose related to 'God's Program' for the world. If you rate God's Program above all of man's efforts, then I highly recommend this book! Using the biblical pattern of recognizing and releasing God's gifts to every believer, David shows how to move us from spectator to participator, from bench warmer to transformer. Remember after Pentecost believers fled the comfort and security of the upper room, then ran into the streets releasing the Holy Spirit to influence every part of the outside world. This revealed God's program then, and He's never changed it, so let's get with the program, "God's program".

—**Rev. Al Rowan**
Pastor/Evangelist/Teacher
Warner Robbins, Georgia

It used to be more difficult to sift out "hidden agendas" in many areas of society and media. Today, it doesn't take nearly the skill to do that, as so many "agendas" are now being shouted from rooftops and presented in all forms as gospel truth. (Never mind, it surely doesn't remotely resemble the Gospel Truth that we understand from God as presented in the Bible!) To offer a hand of hope and some meaningful progress in a world that leaves everyone scratching their heads wondering how much odder can things become, Dr. Dave Robinson, a master of Marketplace Ministry and Leadership Coaching offers a thought-provoking question in his latest read - "Do You Want to Pastor or Transform Your City". Take the time to read Dr. Robinson's message and be sure you understand the difference!

—**Kerry L. Fink DRE CRMC CRSM**
TYG Media, Director
Palm Bay, Florida

"David Robinson arrests you from the first paragraph. He pierces with questions and then states the obvious we have long been blind to. He provides a framework and the priorities to position us for the transformation of our cities. There are multiple veins of gold running through it. If you are currently content or a coward, don't read it; the book will only make you feel responsible. But, if you desire to see the Lord's kingdom making conspicuous advances in our cities and the heart to face our many failed efforts and then take the courage to cooperate with the Lord's victory; then his insights will illuminate with a liberating clarity the challenging gauntlet before us. We have been asleep far too long as we hoped to get carried away out of the culture's chaos. David's book is a trumpet blast, and it is much more. It is a road map with the strategy and key points of emphasis from which we can discover the Lord's decisive points of battle. There is no easy path ahead. But there is divine wisdom and resources to implement the Lord's purposes. David reveals profoundly practical and strength-giving understandings that place us into God's agenda. This book gives us the "glasses" through which we should view the future. If you have the guts to read it once, you will refer to it often; you will search its pages again and again."

—**Michael Massa, Director**
Trailblazer Training LLC
Temple, Texas

As you read this book you can feel the heart of David Robinson. I have served on the board of three different churches and served as treasurer of 2 of them. My good friend David has identified the huge problem of most churches. If the pastor is the one "saving the lost" with the congregation paying him to do so, the church soon plateaus. People are to be taught and trained by the pastor and staff to save the lost. Every pastor, every church leader, every business person, every tradesman, and every person with a heart for the lost should read this. It may change many churches for the Gospel's sake.

—**David Griffith**
Executive VP
Viziv Technologies
Waxahachie, Texas

Good job, David. You have done it again! I always appreciate your love for the lost and suffering humanity and your passion to help pastors and churches to concentrate on winning them. Writings like this are becoming more and more urgent as time comes to a close. Many people will live and die and go to hell forever. We must accept your challenge and take the power of God to the heart of our communities. May this book stir up all of us to activate our witness.

—Dr. Mark Barclay
Pastor, Living Word Church
Founder, Righteous Preachers Network
Midland, Michigan

The Church wants to expand the Kingdom of God on earth but does not have a plan for transforming cities. Coach David challenges the body of Christ to transform cities. We have confused sacred and secular. He states it will take Apostolic leadership to regain the gates of Business, Government and Education. Marketplace ministers are our only hope for the transformation of cities.

—Glenn Repple, Founder
G A Repple and Company
TheReppleMinute.com
Orlando, Florida

I have known Dr. David Robinson for nearly 40 years, he has always pushed the envelope of the local church. In his book, "Do You Want to Pastor or Transform Your City?" He asks this question about the intention of the local church and then lays out an excellent road map based on Scripture of how to transform an entire city. David's passion for the implementation of the five-fold ministry is refreshing and revolutionary in our society and in this "church culture". Many Pastors will teach on the five-fold ministry, but they do not know how to implement it in their church, and thus they are not seeing a transformation in their city. Please do not just read this book and say "that is a great idea" and then carry on as usual. Make sure you read this book and then make the tough decision and do the hard work to put the teaching into practice and see your city transformed.

—Dr Denny Nissley
Christ In Action
Executive Director
Elkwood, Virgina

Just like a good coach, Dr. Robinson begins with a question asking you what you want. If you want transformation, this book is for you. It will teach you as it challenges you. Dr. Robinson's call to church leaders to train and empower marketplace ministers is clear. His warning of what will happen if we don't is dire. And his specific instructions for becoming a city-transforming church are practical.

—Joshua Cole
Certified Life Coach and Pastor
Tabernacle of Praise in Crestline, Ohio

Dr. Robinson's insight is so incredibly simple that we have missed it while searching for the profound. He makes two very clear and scripturally provable points: The first being that a healthy church has represented, in its leadership and in its voices, all five gifted offices of the church; that when a single voice sitting in a single position holds all the power and always holds the microphone, there is lack and it is unhealthy. If we could only drop our ego and our logo at the door, the Kingdom would advance locally and globally by simply applying the simple formula found in Ephesians 4.

Secondly, there is the clear mandate that the church should not and cannot be contained within the walls of our buildings and that the Bible does not teach that there is a delineation between the sacred and the secular. By restricting ministry to Sunday mornings and within our religious structures we have greatly handicapped any progress towards the completion of the Great Commission. Dr. Robinson's challenge to equip every believer to bring the Gospel into the marketplace is a much-needed return to the origins of evangelical thought. This word needs to be shouted from the mountaintop and preached from every pulpit.

—Curt Williams
Executive Director
Youth-Reach, Inc.
Houston, Texas
Summerdale, Alabama

Highly recommended. Do you want to pastor or transform your city is a must read for those that want to be relevant in this dispensation. The book title speaks volumes and the content is eye opening. This is not a book to just read but study. It gives you practical tools on the most critical things to focus on now. This is a new way of thinking about the ministry in our world. Let's touch government, education and business. Thanks a million Coach Dave Robinson.

—**Dr. Richie Achukwu**
Author, Coach and Founder of Prophetic Entrepreneur

DO YOU WANT TO PASTOR, OR TRANSFORM YOUR CITY?

DR. DAVID ROBINSON

Do You Want To Pastor, or Transform Your City?
Copyright © 2022 by Dr. David P. Robinson
First Edition

ISBN: 978-0-9882588-8-4

PUBLISHED BY
CITY LIMITS INTERNATIONAL
PUBLISHERS
CHICAGO, ILLINOIS
2022

Unless otherwise noted, all scripture references are in the New King James Version of the Bible.

Scripture taken from the New King James Version®. Copyright © 1982 by Thomas Nelson. Used by permission. All rights reserved.

Scripture quotations marked (NLT) are taken from the Holy Bible, New Living Translation, copyright ©1996, 2004, 2015 by Tyndale House Foundation. Used by permission of Tyndale House Publishers, Carol Stream, Illinois 60188. All rights reserved.

Scripture quotations taken from the Amplified® Bible (AMPC),
Copyright © 1954, 1958, 1962, 1964, 1965, 1987 by The Lockman Foundation
Used by permission. www.lockman.org

Scripture quotations from King James Bible (KJV). Public Domain

Cover Design:
BrandFlare Creative
www.BrandFlare.net

Printed in the United States of America

TABLE OF CONTENTS

Preaching is informing and creating a sense of urgency for Kingdom concerns. Pastoring is caring for the needs and health of the flock. Both are vital to the mission of the Church. However, neither are frontline issues in the transformation of cities. Cities are made up of people, hurting people that need care. You cannot help but think of Mother Teresa when you think about caring for hurting people. She was known as the 'missionary to the least of the least.' She transformed many lives, but it was Gandhi who led the transformation of India. Pastors ensure healthy warriors.

City Transformation becomes a reality when apostolic leaders develop apostolic congregations whose members gain and hold the moral high ground in their city. Whereas pastors ensure healthy warriors, apostolic leaders turn those warriors into an occupying army with just one thing on their mind, transformation. It's going to take all the Ascension Gifts to experience the full expression of Christ in local congregations. When those local church families unite as the one Ekklesia in the city marketplace, transformation is ripe, and revival has come.

ACKNOWLEDGEMENTS

A big thank you to Jason Gatlin for designing the cover and laying out the book and preparing it for publication. For all of you aspiring Christian authors, Jason is the consummate professional and go to guy for helping you get your book finished and ready for print.

I also want to thank Manna Rose for doing the final line edit and providing some very helpful content suggestions.

DEDICATION

This book is dedicated to my wife, Marie. She has passionately and faithfully served her God and King since she was a young teenager. I have been the beneficiary of that relationship for over 54 years as her husband. Her value to me and our family of three children, eight grandchildren and three great-grandchildren cannot be measured in human terms. She is truly a Proverbs 31 woman, admired by so many around the world who know her best.

FOREWORD

David and Marie strode into our path as friends. As David began to unfold, in simple and enlightening conversations, his wisdom, after having pastored and run a multi-million dollar successful business, we realized what he had to offer was not only friendship, but wisdom we could glean and apply to our own lives.

His skill set, derived from both the non-profit and the business sector, provided experience from both worlds. So each time we were together we asked questions, we listened, and we became wiser...and inspired!

David's knowledge of the scriptures and their application simply poured out of his being...they were part of his everyday conversation, and we knew his wisdom needed to be captured and shared with others.

As he shared his passion to transform cities with the recognition that EVERYONE is called to the work of the ministry—every plumber, lawyer, teacher, pastor, administrator, parent—we realized this revelation had to be shared NOW—especially in this celebrity culture where platform leaders are often thought of as "in the ministry" and the rest of us are simply working at a job.

Instead, David began with the premise that if you are a believer, you are CALLED into ministry!

This book will enlighten leaders and pastors, managers and administrators, entrepreneurs and CEO's with the magnificent joy that following the Kingdom path God has designed specifically for you is fulfilling, rewarding, and brings fruit for the Kingdom.

By empowering every believer to understand they, too, can make an impact with their life, the exponential effectiveness of the Gospel implemented in everyday life can revolutionize a business, a ministry, a church, a business, and your city.

Enjoy the revelation in the following pages of this book…and embrace the adventure!

—Ray and Christy Wilkerson
MAOZ Israel Ministries
Former VP of Ministry Partnerships
and International Administrator

INTRODUCTION

Through his book, Dr. David Robinson has brought continued clarity to my calling. He has helped me with the ability to advance as the effective and confident leader that I am today.

Over ten years ago, I was a wide-eyed and novice leader with many questions, one who felt a passionate and inward drive to bridge both pastoral ministry and community chaplaincy. Yet, I found no easy path and many times much tension from church leadership for me to choose between either/or – to be one or the other – the church pastor or the community chaplain.

I then discovered that God's calling specific to me could and should be lived out as and/both, and that there is a Biblically ordered mission for the Church of Jesus Christ today to be a present help. For me in real time, this looked like finding impactful, creative, and yes sometimes new and unconventional ways to forge paths amidst an ever-changing world landscape. For me, I wanted to be a Church leader who would attempt to be just as effective in the marketplace as inside the Church building.

Sadly today, we are seeing some of the strongest cultural currents unfolding which desire to remove the presence of God, Church, the fabric of our families and Christian parenthood farther and farther away.

This book and Dr. Robinson help tackle the need for cultural transformation and the dire need for leadership empowerment through the Ephesians 4 giftings.

As leaders, we can take inventory of who we are, what we've been called to do, and how we can confidently equip Apostolic congregations, teams, and marketplace leaders for transformational ministry today.

Christians must reclaim the Christian worldview to define our culture, and Dr. Robinson determines that this can be accomplished by possessing the influential gates of business, government and education by possessing the gates of our enemy which is Biblical (Genesis 22:17; 24:60).

In this book, he presents the need for a fundamental change in Church leadership to accomplish this goal of transformation. Who are those best suited to affect this change?

His answer lies in utilizing the Ascension Gifts, all five working together with the Apostolic gift leading the cause for transformation. We read that the mission of the apostolic gifting is to make disciples, and the mission of church leadership is to equip the saints for ministry. Dr. Robinson advocates that it is through bold and confident marketplace ministers that we will be able to infiltrate the gates of our enemy and reclaim them for Christ.

Many leaders today can and should rethink how our efforts not only are to strengthen the Church from within, but also how each of us can place an equal if not greater priority for pursuing onramps and opportunities into business, education, and government.

Dr. Robinson lays out and shows how one can be an effective Luke 9 & 10 marketplace minister. This book is a must read for every Christian organizational leader desiring to be a change agent, for one exploring a call to ministry, or for anyone with a passion to advance the cause for Christ.

—Dr. Loretta Iannicelli
Founder & President
Equip Church | Academy | Care Ministries
Boston, Massachusetts

CHAPTER ONE

PASTORING
OR TRANSFORMING?

I guess the questions must be asked: Do you want to pastor your city, or do you want to transform your city? Do you want to provide for the shepherding needs of your city, or do you want to transform the marketplace where all spiritual battles for dominant influence are won or lost? Are you providing sheep who are healthy and well fed, or are you training Kingdom Warriors that are possessing the gates (places of influence) in your city?

How you answer these questions will not only determine your passion for what's to come in this book, but also the ministry strategy with which you approach the battle between the Kingdom of Light and the kingdom of darkness for control of your city.

If you have the title, position, gifting, and function of pastor, you have a wonderful gift that is critical to the people of God. As it was in Jesus's day, the masses are hurting and wandering about as sheep without a shepherd, like Scripture says. The Church cannot create an army of warriors out of wounded, broken, and hurting people. To report for duty on the frontlines of spiritual warfare you must be reasonably healthy and able to stand the rigors of training and development.

That is the role of the pastor/shepherd along with the teacher. This role cannot be discounted in any way. God's army must be healthy before any level of effective warfare can be waged, much less before victories are won. The first gift a new Christian must meet is that of pastor. It's the pastor who meets them at the altar of sin-sacrifice that helps them get healed from sin and the effects of a sinful lifestyle.

However, to become a warrior that can take on the enemy of Christ and the Church requires the input of the other four Ephesians 4 gifts. Only the full expression of Christ can win the victory in the day of battle. The role of church leadership is to equip the saints for ministry. Church work is what goes on inside our facilities and at our gatherings. The work of the Church is what happens in the public square, the marketplace.

For the Church to have prophetic marketplace influence and effectively address the biblical purpose for God's people expressed in Genesis 22:17 and 24:60 as well as the assigned mission in Matthew 28:18-20, she must embrace the priesthood of all Believers, not a small select group.

The purpose of Jesus's coming was to destroy the works of the devil, the evil one. Though he does act up at times in church, the devil's main activity takes place in the marketplace. The purpose of salvation and Holy Spirit baptism was to transform the marketplace, the place where most lost people go every day. The coming of Jesus to the earth, followed by the Holy Spirit on the Day of Pentecost, was not to swell the church roles, but to win lost souls and transform cities and nations.

The bible says in Psalms 2:8, "Ask of me and I will give you the nations for your inheritance." This was the precursor to the command in Matthew to disciple all nations. I can assure you that those nations don't come easy and require a lot of resources.

Winning the lost and turning them into frontline warriors requires more than the pastoral gift. It requires the full complement of Christ's gifts laid out in Ephesians 4 along with a clear understanding of God's purpose for His people: "You will possess the gates of your enemy." (Genesis 22:17)

You cannot disciple a nation until you possess the places of influence. Until bold, confident marketplace ministers infiltrate the "gates of influence" that control every city, state, and nation, they remain the stronghold of the enemy. The Business Gate pays for everything. The Government Gate controls everything through laws and regulations. The Educational Gate determines the values, philosophy, and worldview that business and government leaders use every day to make determinations.

Our marketplace ministers must not only infiltrate these gates of influence, but they must also allow God's favor to elevate them through the value they bring to their ministry assignment, rising to the level of dominant influence. Once in this place of influence, they must model Christian values and lead every day as Jesus would.

Church leader, you must train your marketplace leaders not to be a Political Action Committee influencing these gates of influence as activists promoting some type of Liberation Theology. God has not called the Church to change its marketplace culture through pressure, endorsements, or public displays. None of these are necessarily wrong; they're just not God's assignment for the Church. Our mission as Christians is being salt and light while gathering the harvest of future harvesters.

Possessing the Gates of the Enemy

"...that in blessing I will bless thee, and in multiplying I will multiply thy seed as the stars of the heaven, and as the sand which is upon the seashore; and thy seed shall possess the gate of his enemies;" —Genesis 22:17 (KJV)

"And they blessed Rebekah and said to her, 'Our sister, may you become thousands of ten thousands, and may your offspring possess the gate of those who hate him!" —Genesis 24:60 (ESV)

It seems that marketplace leadership is suffering from moral AIDS. The integrity to resist sin is gone. Regardless of your eschatology, every generation must confront evil in the marketplace of their day. The Gospel not only has the power to save people from their sin, but also to empower them to change the culture and possess the places of influence, leading to the discipling of entire nations.

Without intentionality, and without church leaders training their people to be not only servants within their spiritual family, but frontline Kingdom Warriors running toward and defeating the Goliaths of their day, it won't happen. Historically, it seems God's people surrender too often and too willingly their God-given rightful place of authority and influence—the power of Tsaddiguim, the Hebrew word for righteous.

When righteous people are in power, the Bible says the people rejoice. When evil people are in power, the people mourn. Scripturally, there is no question God that wants righteous people to be in places of authority and to possess the gates of influence.

The gates of the Old Testament cities were places of influence. Issues of mercy, judgement, righteousness, education, and business were discussed and decided by the elders in the gates. Today, the righteous are not only unwelcome in places of influence and authority, but are also mocked and disdained. There was a time in America when the Judeo-Christian ethic and morality ruled, but no longer. It seems that Isaiah's prophecy has come true:

"Our courts oppose the righteous, and justice is nowhere to be found. Truth stumbles in the streets, and honesty has been outlawed."
—*Isaiah 59:15 (NLT)*

When the New Testament writers were looking for a word to describe first-century believers, they chose the word ekklesia—"the called-out ones". Other words were available, but they chose from the Septuagint, the Old Testament translated into Greek. The assembly of the righteous in the Old Testament is now the assembled Church in the New Testament marketplace.

The Body of Christ is most scattered on Sundays when it meets in its local congregations. It is most gathered on Mondays when it ministers in the marketplace. Church pastor/leader, you must prepare them for both places. For its first 150 years, it was the Church that held the places of influence in America—business, government, and education—but no longer.

To prove it, you have to look no further than the laws that were passed to remove prayer and Bible reading from the classrooms, the rewriting of school textbooks, and open support of sinful lifestyles.

Places of Influence God Promised Abraham

What are the places of influence, the controlling gates God promised Abraham and his seed (you and I) would possess? First, the Business Gate. According to Deuteronomy 8:18, it's the Lord our God who gives the power to create wealth. Any ability or talent first comes from God before it can be developed into a strength. There are people, sinners, who have a gift for which they give God no credit. However, it does not diminish their ability to create wealth.

As believers we know the power to create wealth was given by God to establish His covenant on the earth. This is the challenge for Christian businesspeople—to win others to Christ and have them working for the Kingdom of Light.

Without resources, there is no sustainable ministry. Church leaders must never forget: Your businesspeople are not with you to be your private ATM to fund all your church projects. They want to and will support you, but you are called by God to equip them for the call they have to create wealth and have influence in the world of business. The more the keepers of the Business Gate prosper, the more the Kingdom of God advances.

Second, the Government Gate. These are our God-ordained legislators. They pass the laws and regulations that control our society and culture. I've heard church leaders all my life advise to stay out of politics. It's corrupted and dirty. Pray for them, yes, but don't get involved.

How did politics become so corrupt and evil? The Church walked away and was no longer a part. Sad to say, corrupt church leaders and an out-of-control humanistic government have been in bed together for the past 80 years. High-profile evangelical leaders refuse to take on the battle publicly while preaching a cultur- ally-compromising Gospel. If you want to know where evil politicians are taking us, simply read the Humanist Manifesto I and II.

Third, the Education Gate. Our educators determine the values, philosophy, and worldview of every succeeding generation. According to the writers of "None Dare Call It Education" and "Bending the Twig", our children's education is no longer primarily learning the arts and sciences, but indoctrination.

The National Educators Association, or NEA, America's strongest and wealthiest union, is determined to obliterate every visage of God, Christianity, and the Bible out of the classroom. It is well funded and has made it its life's purpose to indoctrinate our children with anti-God philosophy until they can no longer see any difference between right or wrong. There is no absolute truth; it's all relative. Truth is what you believe it to be, regardless of how much harm and heartache that brings.

Why Are We Not Possessing the Gates of Our Enemy?

"For the kingdom of heaven is like a landowner who went out early in the morning to hire laborers for his vineyard. Now when he had agreed with the laborers for a denarius a day, he sent them into his vineyard. And he went out about the third hour and saw others standing idle in the marketplace, and said to them, 'You go also into the vineyard, and whatever is right I will give you.' So they went. Again he went out about the

sixth and ninth hour, and did likewise. And about the eleventh hour he went out and found others standing idle, and said to them, 'Why have you been standing here idle all day?' They said to him, 'Because no one hired us.' He said to them, 'You also go into the vineyard, and whatever is right you will receive.'" —Matthew 20:1-7 (NKJV)

The Church goes to the marketplace every day. Some Christians still think they have secular jobs, and some have had the revelation they no longer have a job, but a calling and a ministry. Church leader, it's up to you to help them understand the difference. You will never see the transformation of your city as long as you keep sending laypeople to secular jobs in the marketplace.

When Constantine became Emperor of Rome, the Church began to buy into Cessationism and certain gifts and experiences critical to the Early Church and the advancement of Christianity ceased. As a result, church leaders started teaching poor marketplace theology while creating a class system using such terms such as clergy, laity, full-time, part-time, bi-vocational, and other non-biblical designations. Much of which has led to the Church having little significant influence where it's needed most, in the harvest field we call the marketplace.

Ephesians 4 has great implications for marketplace ministry. There are those God has called to train and equip His warriors, and there are those He has called to execute His strategies to reap the harvest and build an ever-increasing army to possess the gates of their enemy.

Neither role is more or less significant and critical to the task. It should not be an either-or choice.

Ministry should not be about geography or location but calling and awareness, whether it's in the church house, office, shop, or classroom. The Apostle Paul in Hebrews said not to forsake assembling together. However, Jesus said to go into the highways and byways.

In the Matthew 20 text, the laborers seemed more concerned about wages than activity. Pastor, it's up to you to persuade your marketplace ministers that the harvest must always be the motivation for going out to the fields every day, not monetary gain. The Greek word for idle in Matthew 20:6 is argos, meaning "free from labor, at leisure, lazy, and shunning the work that has been assigned". As church leaders, you can't train them for the *job* to which God has called them, but you can surely equip them for Kingdom ministry while they are there.

Another reason for idleness in the marketplace is that the Church is confused about the difference between marketing the Gospel and evangelism. Marketing is creating a sense of urgency and increasing demand. Evangelism, sales, is closing the deal. The Church has tried to create a sense of urgency in the church house but has been unable to close the transaction in the marketplace.

With few exceptions, church leaders do not adequately prepare their members for evangelism or possess a clear strategy for taking back influence in the marketplace of their city. It's admirable to reach out and meet the social and spiritual needs of your city, but the purpose of your church in your city is transforming the culture, changing it from an anti-God and humanistic influence to one that glorifies God and establishes His covenant promises.

The pastor/teacher gifts alone cannot produce that transformation. Transformation does not take place until all five Ephesians 4 gifts work together under the leadership of the apostolic gift. I have little use for titles and offices if they do not advance the Kingdom message and mission. Too often they have been used to gain power and prestige and to put Christians in bondage, while accomplishing very little in transforming cities and discipling nations.

A title and name plaque on your office door does not guarantee the gift is present. Only the gift produces significant and sustainable fruit.

Only the Ascension Gifts Provide Full Expression of Christ

Ephesians 4 teaches that in the Ascension Gifts reside the full expression of Christ. He is the sum total of apostle, prophet, evangelist, pastor, and teacher. Since Christ is Head of the Church and the Church is His body and in Him "we live and move and have our being", it makes sense that every local assembly would want to reflect His wholeness, first within their own fellowship and then with those the Holy Spirit schedules divine appointments every day.

The Holy Spirit came not only to teach us more about Christ and to empower us to serve His body, but also to empower us to show His love to the world. All through the Gospels, the Early Church demonstrated the fullness of Christ through Spirit-empowered, gifted believers. For the first 300 years, the growth and development of the "called out ones" centered around fully embracing and exercising these five supernatural gifts as living witnesses.

Today's Church is not lacking titles and positions but saints who know their gifting and how to use it in serving their spiritual family, communicating God's love, and finishing His mission. Education, personality, and passion may enhance your gift, but they do not determine it. Even surrounding needs do not determine your gift. Only God determines your gift. And it's your gift that determines where you are most effective, meet the most needs, and have the greatest Kingdom influence.

God's calling on your life will always exploit the gift He gave you. Frustrated, weary and restless Christians are usually trying to serve God outside their gifting. Both in the Body and the marketplace. No amount of effort and perseverance or even a change of geography will overcome these feelings. The joy, peace, and fulfillment so desired in our calling comes from doing what God has gifted us to do, not what others think we ought to do.

The level of effectiveness of any local assembly is determined by the apostolic gift, regardless of what title they give their leader. It's the apostolic gift building and supporting the other four gifts that brings strength, maturity, and unity and produces a battle-ready army. Equipping the saints without understanding their gift breeds redundancy and disappointment at best, and at worst, confusion and mission failure. When a local church is deficient or impotent in any given area, rest assured it's lacking in the gift God assigned to meet that need.

Without the apostolic gift, you have an unfathered church. One lacking a compelling vision and strategic leadership.

Without the prophetic gift, you have an uncorrected church. One lacking discipline; unruly and unable to handle correction.

Without the teaching gift, you have an untaught church. One lacking a strong biblical foundation while partial truths and false doctrine abound.

Without the pastoral gift you have an "un-shepherded" church. One lacking compassion, spiritual healing, and a sense of family.

Without the evangelist gift you have an unpopulated church. One lacking passion for the lost and a steady flow of new converts.

The evangelist cares about how many say "yes" to Jesus. The pastor cares about how many are receiving care for hurts and wounds. The teacher cares about how many are growing in the Word and faith. The prophet cares about how many are living holy. The apostle cares about it all and builds a team to ensure it happens. Evangelism is where it all starts.

However, without all five gifts operating in harmony, you are simply populating an army that has sons without fathers, is living in rebellion, lacks biblical understanding, is broken and hurting, and cannot reproduce itself.

Jesus said, "I will build my church (using all five gifts) and the gates (places of influence) of hell will not prevail." (Matthew 16:18)

Jesus repeatedly uses the term marketplace but somehow the Church continually fails to comprehend how important it is to world evangelism and discipling the nations. Jesus refused to involve Himself in the ecclesiastical system and seemed to go out of His way to avoid it.

Early church leaders, especially the Apostle Paul, were anything but idle in the marketplace. By the third century, institutional concerns took precedence over efforts to impact the marketplace in any significant way. Indoor church meetings led by religious managers found a way to keep everyday Christians busy in the building, and their marketplace activities and influence became less and less. Note Jesus's words:

> "'To what can I compare the people of this generation?' Jesus asked. 'How can I describe them? They are like children playing a game in the public square. They complain to their friends, "We played wedding songs, and you didn't dance, so we played funeral songs, and you didn't weep." For

John the Baptist did not spend his time eating bread or drinking wine, and you say, "He's possessed by a demon." The Son of Man, on the other hand, feasts and drinks, and you say, "He's a glutton and a drunkard, and a friend of tax collectors and other sinners!"'" —Luke 7:31-34 (NLT)

Jesus was describing the religious leaders of His day as children sitting around in the marketplace complaining. They didn't have a clue who John or Jesus were and why they came. It seems we have a similar situation today. The Church goes to great lengths to describe and define our anti-Christ culture but lacks any clear strategy on how to change it. The prophets keep predicting what God's going to do someday according to Scripture, but the apostolic gift is silent on how marketplace ministers, the warriors who go to the frontlines every day, can affect change.

Ezekiel went to great lengths in describing marketplace activities in Tyre, the center of economic activity, and how God's people were falling down on the job. Today's Church seems to be more interested with advertising what's happening inside their walls while neglecting marketplace opportunities all around them. Marketing internal church activities does little in creating marketplace activity. Our enemy is not the least bit concerned with the size of our meeting facilities, how many attend our meetings, or the size of our institutional budget.

What does threaten his kingdom of darkness is how many well-trained warriors the Church sends to invade and take back the ground that rightfully belongs to our

King, the King of Righteousness. Promoting church events should never replace our passion for marketplace influence and destroying the works of the devil.

Invading the darkness and gathering the harvest should be a way of life, not an occasional event. Marketing the Kingdom of Light searches out the unreached people or group. Evangelism communicates the uncompromised message in a relevant way. Discipleship completes the transaction and creates a lifetime follower of Jesus Christ.

True evangelism shares the Gospel with those who have never heard. It's the revivalist that travels from church to church stirring up the saints. Gifted evangelists seldom travel, yet their schedule remains full. We call it marketplace evangelism.

Church leaders, your main calling is to energize your idle marketplace warriors. Most don't know what to do, how to do it, or even why they go into the marketplace outside of earning an income to support their family and the church they attend. Most cannot see a direct correlation between what they hear on Sundays and what they face on Mondays.

Traditional church models and leaders must change that, or marketplace ministers remain idle and the laborers for Kingdom advancement remain unemployed. Your marketplace ministers have been called to one of three places of service: business, government, or education. It's your job to help them find God's purpose for being there and how to be effective.

You must help them stop compartmentalizing their lives into "secular vs. sacred". Those compartments don't exist in God's world, and they shouldn't in ours. Your life as a church leader and their lives as marketplace ministers must be the integration of God-given opportunities woven into a seamless life lived to the glory of God, regardless of where you live out your priesthood.

The Bible says our whole life was planned before we were born, and our steps are ordered of the Lord for His service. If that is the case, how can we have both secular and sacred parts to our lives? I believe this kind of thinking has done more to hold back world evangelism and fulfilling the Church's purpose and mission more than any other single reason.

How Many Lights
Does a Lighting Store Need?

Richard Halverson, Chaplain, United States Senate 1981-94, made the following quote in his book "Walk Between Sunday":

"The Church has succeeded in pulling Christians out of the world, out of society   and out of civic affairs. So often the Church is a little island of piety surrounded   by an ocean of need. Our preoccupation with the establishment has been so complete that we have been unable to see the ocean. Except of course, if there   is someone out there that we want to recruit for our program. The congregation has become an exclusive little system of satellites orbiting our programs."

How many lights does a lighting store need? The biblical goal of the informed church leaders managing the "lighting store" is producing spiritually and emotionally mature warriors who take their place as lights in a dark world. Ambassadors in a hostile environment. Messengers to an uninformed society. Hope dealers to a hopeless society. And M.D.s—Mighty Deliverers—to the sick, wounded and devastated.

The question is not how involved you are using your lamp in the lighting store, or if you light up every time the store is open. The question should be how well the leaders of your church lighting store are equipping you to use your lamp to light up the dark areas where you go every week in the marketplace. If they aren't fulfilling their Ephesians 4 assignment, why do you continue to follow?

Church leaders must continue to produce people whose ordinary stations in life are transformed into opportunities to share the love of God and extend His Kingdom principles throughout the earth, resulting in the discipling of all nations. This cannot be accomplished in one or two meetings a week, or even every night of the week, or by a handful of professionals. Every believer has not only been called, gifted, and assigned to reach the lost and disciple them in the Word, but they must also be trained in the art of spiritual warfare, executed from their platform of marketplace ministry.

"A city set on a hill cannot be hidden. Nor do men light a lamp and hide it under a bushel, but on a lampstand so it gives light." —Matthew 5:14-15

Visibility is always the issue. How many lamps do you need in a lighting store? Not many, but every Christian is called to shine where it's darkest. Church leader, it's your God-given assignment to help them make that happen. Marketplace ministers, your marketplace calling is your lampstand. Make sure you are not a flashlight used only in emergencies. Don't be a strobe light—lots of glitter, but inconsistent at best.

Mature Christians are searchlights, not looking for sin in peoples' lives, but showing them a path out of the darkness, disappointment, and despair common to so many God brings across their path every day. This only happens when the lamps leave the lighting store and leave their light on.

I have been developing leaders, building teams, and finding solutions in both the church world and the marketplace for many years. I've seen God draw men's souls to the message of the Cross and do signs and wonders in both of these places. In this book I have shared my heart, and I pray that the message reaches yours.

The Bible says that the harvest is great but that laborers, those who understand why God called them to the marketplace, are few. It's time we affirm, develop, and deploy the 95 percent who will never fill a pulpit. They have a call and a platform in the marketplace: the first-century mission field and the 21st century's greatest opportunity.

I close Part One with some practical ways you can make your Church Ephesians 4:1 friendly:

• Map your city or area indicating where your E41 ministers live out their Ephesians 4:1 assignment.

• Schedule regular onsite visits with your E41 ministers for support and encouragement.

• Have "How I Connect Sunday to Monday" testimonies often.

• Develop a solid biblical theology for work and marketplace ministers. Teach and preach on it regularly.

• Commission your E41 ministers after their training in a special service.

• Conduct an annual "Marketplace Ministers" conference and a Sunday where everyone comes dressed in their ministry uniforms.

• Put the tools of Ephesians 4:1 ministers on display as a way of honoring them and their calling.

• Discontinue dismissing your services and instead release them to ministry.

• Install signs over all exit doors reading "Service Entrance".

These are just a few ways you can recognize and affirm those who answer the Ephesians 4:1 call, go through the training, and go to the frontlines every day. Ask God to give you more creative ways to encourage, affirm and support these great men and women. I salute you for all efforts to extend God's Kingdom.

CHAPTER TWO

STRATEGY FOR MARKETPLACE TRANSFORMATION

Transformation begins with anointed marketplace ministers. For a city to be transformed, the marketplace must be transformed. The marketplace is where the battle for our cities is fought and won or lost. There is an army already in place that needs to be recognized, commissioned, and empowered. They have mistakenly been identified as laypeople when in fact they are called and Holy Spirit-empowered marketplace ministers.

Whether they run corporations or work for them, serve in the halls of government, or educate our children and youth in the classrooms of our schools, they are better positioned than vocational church leaders to transform the marketplace—which leads to city trans-formation. Christians in the marketplace already have an anointing to share the Gospel with the lost; but in most cases, the anointing has not been activated, as the laypeople have been relegated to second-class status in the Church.

The Holy Spirit did not come to be a labor-saving device, but a labor-enhancing partner. He comes alongside as our Comforter and Guide, not as a replacement for excellence in teaching, training, team development, and plain old hard work and leadership discipline.

God did not build the Ark; He provided Noah with the vision, tools, and strength to do the work. He didn't kill Goliath as a result of David's praying and singing; He prepared David on the hills of Judea before calling him to the battlefield. Supernatural preparation is just as important, if not more important, on the practice field than it is when facing live opponents on game day.

Anointing is for leveraging what God gifted you to be and do. If you want to enter and win the Kentucky Derby, you must have a thoroughbred. If you want to go to the bottom of the Grand Canyon and return, you need a dependable mule. Both are extremely valuable in their context. Organizations get in trouble when they ignore this reality. The Prophet Samuel could have anointed any of Jesse's sons. However, he only anointed the one God called and gifted with the leadership gifts to lead Israel, not just whoever could kill her enemies.

Prophetic impact in the marketplace is the Church's best hope for world evangelism and finishing the Matthew 28 mandate. Marketplace missions is the primary mission field on every continent in the 21st century. As the world shrinks via technology and diminishing travel times, it only increases the urgency for the

Church to have primary influence in the marketplace. Globalization in all aspects economic, political, social, environmental and most of all spiritual demands the Church rethink its approach to world evangelism.

Marketplace Ministers
Are the Only Hope

Integration of faith and work demands a three-pronged approach. The integration of faith and work *in light of globalization* requires a theology for marketplace missions. This theology must include how the Word, the Church and the marketplace relate, complement, and integrate in the lives of believers through personal experience.

So, marketplace missions theology demands a three-pronged approach: First, the Church needs a workable, affordable, and effective plan for gaining and maintaining a viable presence in the marketplace. The Church must have significant influence, prophetic impact and transformation as her goal. Effective marketplace ministers are the only hope for this to happen.

Second is contextualization of the Gospel in the marketplace. It simply means understanding the context or realities where you are trying to share the Gospel. If the audience cannot understand your message, it matters little what you say or how loud or long you say it.

Third, biblical theology for marketplace missions must be simple, clear, and comprehensive. Training marketplace ministers and missionaries requires a biblical understanding of contemporary marketplace issues. There are issues specific to business, government, and educational arenas, while there are issues common to all three.

> **KEY:** *Globalization, Christian worldview, moral capitalism, materialism, consumerism, the question of when life begins, and a myriad of other issues are challenging our marketplace ministers. Sadly, many church leaders stand strangely silent about most of these issues. We must include a curriculum and training opportunities that prepare marketplace ministers for the realities they face every day. If they are openly Christian, the resistance and growing hostility is more than many are prepared to face, much less go to battle against and win.*

The Difference Between Marketplace Ministers and Missionaries

Marketplace mission theology must include an understanding of three marketplace ministry dynamics. First, the marketplace is a blend of business, government, and education. These three entities control every nation and then the entire world.

Second, marketplace ministry is not a secondary mission or calling. 90 percent or more of the Church has this calling (Matthew 28). And third, the Church's mission is more than making better church members; it is producing more effective marketplace ministers. They bring revival to the marketplace, not just the church house (Joel 2:28; Acts 2:17-21).

This theology must also distinguish between marketplace ministers and marketplace missionaries. Ministers are those called to the marketplace by vocational calling. Missionaries are those sent to the marketplace on a specific mission.

Full-time marketplace ministers of the Gospel are never part-time or bi-vocational. Pulpit or marketplace, the anointing is the same (Acts 2:4). They have a call, not a job. They need taught, trained, empowered, commissioned, and affirmed in that ministry calling.

Jesus is our model. He was a small business owner. He called 12 marketplace men, trained them, and sent them back to the marketplace. None left their marketplace "calling" to go into full-time ministry. His teaching and training covered marketplace missions; he taught very little about church life.

To Jesus there was no secular/sacred divide. Bi-vocational ministry is an oxymoron. It was unheard of among those Early Church believers. His life validated marketplace missions. Even though Jesus was considered a rabbi, none of His disciples were viewed as leaders in the temple or synagogue; Paul being the exception, but only until his Damascus Road encounter.

Bridging the Gap

Marketplace missions must bridge gaps. Gaps between rich and poor. The sick and the whole.

Prejudices and acceptance. The lost and the saved. God is God of the marketplace, not just the Church. The Church must mean more than a building. If not, you can only be the Church when you have a building. You can only have church inside four walls.

Jesus spoke more about the Kingdom than the Church. He referred to the Church twice and the Kingdom 136 times. According to Matthew 28, the mission is extending Kingdom influence and principles to every nation. The best way is through marketplace missions conducted by the Ekklesia.

Local churches are established based on the demand created in the marketplace and for the purpose of supporting the mission. Every local church centers their efforts around the core values laid out in Acts 2:42-47. For too long, it has been the other way around. If the Church does not encounter and defeat the enemy on his ground, the marketplace, he will attack the Church on her turf, the gatherings inside her buildings.

The book of Acts records at least 39 power encounters. All but one took place in the marketplace. It is worth noting that when Israel would not send someone to fight Goliath, he came to them (I Samuel 17:23-25).

Notice where he stood in verse eight: "He stood and cried unto the armies of Israel." Note the change in verse 25: "'Have you seen this man who has come up?'" Goliath has now crossed over the ravine and started up toward the armies of Israel.

The Church must stay on the offensive in the marketplace and not just in her church meetings. In the last 75 years in the USA the Church has surrendered ground she held for so long in the marketplace. Now the marketplace wants the Church back in her building—not in our schools, government, or the public square.

What is an Effective Marketplace Minister?

Steps for being an effective Luke 9 & 10 marketplace minister:

- Be a Christian worthy of your marketplace calling (Ephesians 4:1).
- Know and execute Kingdom principles in your place of ministry with wisdom and without compromise. Jesus was active and intentional in every area of public life.
- Do marketplace missions with an Acts 1:8 and 2:4 dynamic.
- Be committed to Matthew 28 marketplace transformation. Do not settle for just participating and having influence. Be satisfied with nothing less than transformation.

To appreciate marketplace missions, you must notice the difference between the Twelve and the Seventy. The Twelve wanted to change the Temple system and restore the Kingdom back to Israel. Jesus sent the Seventy to change their world by establishing Kingdom influence and principles through the marketplace that would affect all nations.

The Twelve wanted to send the crowds away, build tabernacles, call fire down if necessary, and keep Jesus for their own selfish ambitions. Jesus overruled all their petty issues and called the Seventy to model for the Twelve what He really wanted. Jesus said, "I am sending you out as sheep among wolves." (Luke 10:3) Sheep usually run from wolves, but they listened to His specific instruction:

Speak peace to the wolves – Luke 10:5

Eat and drink what they set before you – Luke 10:7

Care for their needs – Luke 10:9

Proclaim the Kingdom is near – Luke 10:9

Result: Demons became subject to them. Satan lost his power over the region. If the Church would confront the enemy on his own ground, she would have fewer demons to cast out at church.

> *"Teach us to understand how many days we have, then we will have a heart of wisdom to give you... Fill us in the morning with your lovingkindness. Let us be glad all our days... Let the favor of the Lord our God be upon us. In addition, make the work of our hands stand strong. Yes, make the work of our hands (marketplace ministry) stand strong." —Psalms 90:12, 14, 17b*

City Transformation Is Not Optional

"I have given them the glory that you gave me, that they may be one as we are one: I in them and you in me..."
—John 17:22-23a

Can a city be truly transformed, and the Church regain the moral high ground? It seems like a lofty goal, but one the Body of Christ has been empowered to attain. Today there are at least 200 interconnected cities around the world that are in some form of transformation, according to the International Coalition of Workplace Ministries (ICWM) Workplace Transformation.

These cities are at some level of transformation in every aspect of their public, governmental and business life. Webster's Dictionary defines transformation as "to change in nature, disposition, heart, or the like; to convert; a thorough or radical change".

A transformed city is the answer to Jesus's prayer: "Your kingdom come, Your will be done on earth as it is in heaven." (Matthew 6:10) It is God's kingdom manifested here on Earth. What does a transformed city look like? It is one where Kingdom values prevail in business, government, and education.

Marketplace Ministry Leaders Are Key to City Transformation

One of the first cities in the Bible to be transformed was Sychar in Samaria when the Samaritan woman met Jesus at the town well in John 4:7-26. When Jesus revealed to the woman that He knew she had had five husbands, she was amazed and came to believe in Him. She shared her newfound faith with others in the city, and "Many of the Samaritans from that town believed in Him because of the woman's testimony." (John 4:39)

One of the first things that must take place for a city to be transformed is that Jesus must be invited into that city through the city "gatekeepers", those that dominate the places of influence. This is what happened in Sychar and what is happening in cities where transformation is taking place today through bold impassioned market-place ministers.

One such city is Kampala in Uganda, where I have invested much time and energy. At one point, 33.3 percent of the population of Uganda had AIDS. The World Health Organization predicted that the nation's economy would collapse by the year 2000 because there would be only widows and orphans left.

So, people sought the Lord and prayed. The results? Marketplace ministry leaders invited Jesus into their city to be Lord over it. Christians have replaced the evil dictatorship of Idi Amin, whose brutality in the 1970s led to the executions of hundreds of thousands of people and plunged the nation into chaos and poverty.

Today, the people in Parliament pray, the police fax prayer requests to judges, and a major bank even plays praise music on all 11 of their floors. In some communities, crime is down 70 percent and AIDS has dropped to five percent. It's not perfect, but it has come a long way.

The second key is that the cities must repent of their sins. Jesus went into the cities and did great miracles. Yet many of those cities did not repent, and this angered the Lord. "Then Jesus began to denounce the cities in which most of his miracles had been performed, because they did not repent." (Matthew 11:20)

Marketplace ministry leaders are critical to city transformation when they serve in places of influence and have authority to make changes. After years of investment by the Church in the cities of America and others around the world, secular humanists still reign in places of authority.

I believe that is because the wrong gift has led the Church most of time since Constantine became Emperor of Rome and turned the ecclesiology of the Church upside down. The pastoral gift is a vital part of the ministry team, but that gift will never lead a transformational movement strong enough to change a city.

Pastor/teacher-gifted leaders have never held authority in the cities where change needs to originate. Business, government, and educational leaders hold that authority. Until those with the apostolic gift lead in the Church and train and empower those marketplace ministers with the same gift and release them in the public square, we will never see our cities transformed.

All Business Must Be Kingdom Business

Dawie Spangenberg and his wife, Isebel, lead a worldwide prayer initiative called Transformation Africa. He once made a startling comment to a Christian workplace lunch group in Atlanta: "If a business owner is operating a business in a city and is not directly involved in transforming that city, he is raping that city. He needs to leave that city!"

These are strong words, but Spangenberg is convinced that business leaders need to stop trying to see what a business can do for them and start determining why God gave them their business. Then they should seek to build the Kingdom of God in their city. God has gifted them according to Deuteronomy 8:18 to create the wealth that funds both government and education.

The problem that has plagued the Church for centuries is that marketplace ministers are not recognized by vocational church leadership as having a valid calling and true ministry. They have not seen their careers as holy callings and have not understood the redemptive nature of their work (ministry).

Consequently, they often resign themselves to being financiers of God's work instead of being major catalysts for transformation of their workplaces and cities. And yet, when a man or a woman becomes willing to be used in the context of the workplace, God can bring revival and transformation to the city.

Jeremiah Lanphier is a good example of what I'm talking about. He was a businessman in New York City in the mid 1800s. A simple prayer, a willing heart, and an act of obedience resulted in the transformation of cities throughout the United States. Here's his story:

In a small, darkened room in the back of one of New York City's lesser churches, a man prayed alone. His request of God was simple, but earth-shattering: "Lord, what wilt Thou have me to do?"

He was a man approaching midlife, without a wife or family, but he had financial means. He had decided to reject the success syndrome that drove the city's businessmen and bankers. God used this businessman to turn New York City's commercial empire on its head.

He began a businessmen's prayer meeting on September 23, 1857. The meetings began slowly, but within a few months, 20 noonday meetings were convening daily throughout the city. The New York Tribune and the New York Herald issued articles telling of revival. It had become the city's biggest news.

Now a full-fledged revival, it moved outside New York. By spring of 1858, 2,000 men met daily in Chicago's Metropolitan Theatre, and in Philadelphia the meetings mushroomed into a four-month-long tent meeting. Other meetings were held in Baltimore, Washington, Cincinnati, Chicago, New Orleans, and Mobile. Thousands met to pray because one man stepped out. This was an extraordinary move of God through one man.

Learning From a Pioneer

When it comes to city transformation, it is hard to write about the subject without acknowledging Ed Silvoso, founder and president of Harvest Evangelism. He is a modern-day pioneer and a leading authority on the subject. His books "My City God's City", "Prayer Evangelism", and "Anointed for Business" are three must-read titles.

Ed became more involved directly with the workplace movement in 2002 when he saw how important the workplace was to reaching a city. He has discovered four ingredients that must be in place for us to begin to change the spiritual climate in a city. These include:

- Speaking peace to the lost.
- Blessing them, opening the door to unbiased fellowship. Unbiased fellowship establishes a level of trust, allowing our neighbors to share with us their felt needs.
- Taking care of their needs. Prayer addresses these felt needs.
- Proclaiming the Good News. When we intercede for our neighbors, God comes near them in tangible ways.

Ed Silvoso's ministry has a proven history that originates from his work in Resistencia, Argentina. In 1990, this city of 400,000 had an estimated 5,100 believers scattered among 70 congregations (68 of which were the result of a church split).

The city was notorious for being a spiritual cemetery. However, today there are over 100,000 Christians in the city and 220,000 in the province, making it the most evangelical province in the nation. Silvoso reports breakthroughs in Argentina at high levels of government and business.

In the fall of 2004, he made his annual trip to Argentina with a group of marketplace leaders and intercessors. During that trip, the president of a political party received the Lord and invited Jesus to be the head of it. The entire management team of the Argentine equivalent of the Mayo Clinic received the Lord and invited Jesus into the clinic.

The heart of the city is not the Church, much less the church building. The Church is the light of the city, but the heart is the marketplace. Cities are often known by a signature skyline made up of buildings that represent the leading corporations in town. This is where our actions need to be if we are to reach our cities.

The first European convert was a businesswoman who dealt in expensive apparel in Acts 16:14-15. This was immediately followed by a power encounter in the marketplace involving a slave girl with a spirit of divination in verses 16-18. If you want to reach and transform a city, church leaders must inform, empower, and strengthen the army that's on the ground there every day.

Every marketplace warrior must understand their Ephesians 4:1 calling and their Acts 2:4 empowerment. Not just for church work in serving their spiritual family but for their spiritual vocation in the marketplace, the heart of every city.

The enemy is very active and focused on controlling the influence of every city. The Ekklesia needs to be just as focused on her own agenda to gain the hearts of the men and women who will lead those activities.

- Apostolic Ministry Is the Foundation of All Marketplace Ministry Success
- The Apostolic Mandate: "Possess the gates of your enemy (places of influence)." Genesis 22:17 and 24:60
- The Apostolic Mission: "Make disciples of all nations." Matthew 28:19
- The Apostolic Empowerment: "You shall be filled with the Holy Ghost." Acts 2
- The Apostolic Team: "And He gave some to be apostles, prophets, teachers, pastors and evange-lists." Ephesians 4:11
- The Apostolic Fruit: "They that have turned the world upside down have come here also." Acts 17:6b

Apostolic leaders leading apostolic congregations is the only way to transform your city. The Church in America without a doubt needs a prayer-generated reviv-al. However, the purpose of that revival must go beyond having more passionate congregational gatherings.

It must go beyond enlarging our base with new believers and Spirit-filled Church members. It even must go beyond fulfilling the Great Commission of Matthew 28.

It must be about fulfilling the purpose of God's people as promised in Genesis 22:17 and 24:60: possessing the gates of our enemy and those who hate us. Jesus said in Matthew 16:18, "I will build my church and the gates (places of influence) of hell will not prevail against it."

Do you think hell's influence is prevailing in America? Do you think war has been declared on biblical morality and Christianity? The demand for religious pluralism intensifies by the day! Fulfillment of the purpose for which God chose to have a people requires apostolic leaders leading apostolic congregations.

The quantity and quality of apostolic leadership only improves if the process for developing this type of leader is transformed. Academic institutions and traditional training methods are designed to reproduce Bible scholars, shepherds and teachers, but not Kingdom-minded leaders who reproduce competent marketplace ambassadors and spiritual warriors.

Assign whatever title you like to your leaders, but make sure the right gift is the one leading the team and creating training communities that turn out 21st century disciples. The early disciples were not only gripped by the Great Commandment to love one another and love the lost, but they also passionately pursued the gates of their enemy.

They were trained to use the Sword of the Spirit as a weapon of warfare where it counts most—on the frontlines, the marketplace. They were empowered by the Holy Spirit to use their God-given gifts not only in serving the local congregation but in tearing down enemy strongholds and regaining and holding the moral high ground in their city.

Local congregations must go beyond teaching, nurturing, and caring for existing members, as critical as that is to the life of every church family. All congregations must also be involved in gathering the harvest. Evangelism, in most churches, is asking members to share their faith and invite those who show interest to a building called the church. Without apostolic leadership, little happens in the marketplace or the church.

All of this in-house ministry is to prepare, not replace the Church's responsibility to possess the places of influence that control their city. If the Church does not possess these gates of influence, the enemy certainly will, and has.

Apostolic congregations, on the other hand, target the harvest and not the pews. They target the lost in the gates of influence known as business, government, and education. These three gates control your city, your state, and now our nation. Most programs in apostolic congregations target the unchurched, undiscipled and unsaved people in these three gates.

Apostolic leaders and congregations understand and connect the original purpose of God's people with the assignment of the Church in the 21st century. They link that purpose and assignment with the priesthood and giftedness of all believers. Apostolic leaders are in stark contrast to the prevailing church leadership models that a hundred years ago allowed the enemy access to and now full control of America's places of influence.

Jesus Was a Small Business Owner

Apostolic leaders understand that the Founder of the movement we call Christianity was a small business owner most of His life. As a result, He was immersed in and constantly challenged the culture of His day. His recruiting practices reflected His bias. He called people out of the marketplace in order to send them back.

For the Church's first 300 years, preparation for ministry did not involve a credentialing process that removed emerging spiritual leaders from real-life opportunities and challenges found only on the front-lines. If we want America to once again be the light of the world, we must have apostolic leaders that take their cues for ministry from a cultural exegesis as well as a biblical exegesis.

Jesus was the epitome of a leader who did both. He trained His marketplace ministers how to share the Gospel in ways that challenged the unbelievers but also created a desire in them to know more. The Church today must do the same. They must focus more on reaching and developing bold marketplace disciples than building an institution to warehouse the saints until Jesus comes back.

America needs a Church active in the gates of influence and control, not one being shielded from it by a false sense of spirituality and a "come out from among them" separation mentality.

Shepherds, prophets, teachers, and evangelists are all critical to the team's success. However, without apostolic leaders building an apostolic team of those Ephesians 4 gifts leading apostolic congregations, the Church will keep having church but will never be the transforming force God intended. Without apostolic leadership and congregations, regaining the moral high ground and places of influence simply remains a line item on our corporate prayer list, never becoming a reality.

Who are the apostolic leaders in your city Ekklesia? What is their apostolic strategy to gain and hold the moral high ground in the city to which God has called them? Church leaders must not merely have a call to their local congregation's pulpit. Every pulpiteer must have a "call" to not only be a voice for righteousness in their city, but their hearts must also burn with the same passion as John Knox who cried to God in prayer, "Give me Scotland, Lord, or I die."

The Church has long cried out in prayer for revival. However, most revivals that started in seasons of deep intercession in the prayer room have also died in the prayer room, the Church not realizing that the response to prayer is training the army that will execute God's strategy for transformation with the same passion. Once again I ask you, do you want to pastor or transform your city?

DR. ROBINSON'S OTHER BOOKS:

• IDLE IN THE MARKETPLACE AT THE ELEVENTH

HOUR

(Available in Spanish and Audio)

• 50 LEADERSHIP KEYS THAT WORK

• 100 LEADERSHIP NUGGETS

• MESSAGES FROM A FATHER

• POSSESSING THE GATES OF YOUR ENEMY

• THOUGHTS ON THE LORD'S DAY

• THE ABOMNIMABLE SNOWMAN – GOD'S GIFT OF

APOSTOLIC LEADERSHIP TO THE CHURCH

• 52 WEEKS OF WISDOM

CITY LIMITS PUBLISHERS
CHICAGO, ILLINOIS

CONTACT
DR. DAVID ROBINSON

"If you want 'can't fail' leadership prescriptions, hire a consultant. If you want great leadership information, go to a workshop. Do you like learning leadership theory? Sit in a classroom. Do you want to improve your character and life experience? Find a mentor, often called a life coach. However, if you want to be an effective leader, engage a seasoned coach that's been successful in providing winning front-line leadership over the long haul."

Dr. David Robinson
City Limits Ministries International
847-417-8234
c4mcoach@gmail.com
daverobinsoncoach.com

"Developing leaders, building teams, and finding solutions since 1966."

Made in the USA
Monee, IL
12 April 2024

56442646R00039